The Daily Devoted wOman

A Two Week Devotional Guide For
Women To Draw Closer To Christ

DENISE ROTHSTEIN

authorHOUSE®

AuthorHouse™
1663 Liberty Drive
Bloomington, IN 47403
www.authorhouse.com
Phone: 833-262-8899

Published by AuthorHouse 02/06/2019

ISBN: 978-1-5462-7037-9 (sc)
ISBN: 978-1-5462-7036-2 (e)

Library of Congress Control Number: 2018914110

Print information available on the last page.

This book is printed on acid-free paper.

Contents

God's Daily Invitation To You........................vii

Day 1   Dine With Him 1

Day 2   He Calls You By Name 5

Day 3   Come Just As You Are 11

Day 4   Take A Load Off Your Feet....................17

Day 5   Sacrifice Your Time For His Time 21

Day 6   Give Him Your Undistracted Attention 27

Day 7   Keep Calm And Lean On Him 31

Day 8   Listen To Words Of Wisdom...................35

Day 9   Give Him Your Burdens And Lighten Up 40

Day 10 Develop A "Merry" Heart 44

Day 11 Sit And Learn With Your Sisters 48

Day 12 Live A Balanced Devotion To Him..............56

Day 13 The Heart Of The Daily Devoted Woman........60

Day 14 An Eternal And Priceless Treasure..............65

Quick Tips For Fulfilling Devotions....................69

Conclusion...71

God's Daily Invitation To You

"Come to Me all you who are weary and heavy laden and I will give you rest. Take My yoke upon you and learn from Me, for I am gentle and humble in heart, and you will find rest for your souls." Matthew 11:28,29

*W*hat if you had a beautifully crafted invitation addressed specifically to you sitting on your table, ready for you to respond? Most of us would open it with anticipation and carefully read it so we get the right information on the who, what, where, why and when of the invitation.

God is daily sending out His loving invitation to you. It's an invitation meant for a response. If you say yes and open the door of your heart daily to Him, you will find that He is waiting for you to come to Him, sit at His feet, and learn from Him. The *Who* of the invitation is God. The *what* is an intimate relationship with you. The *where* is a place you set apart each day just for drawing near to Him and having devotional time with Him. The *why* is because He loves you and wants to reveal Himself to you, to comfort you, and guide you. The *when* is every day.

We see a picture of a woman who chose to draw near

to the Lord in the story of Jesus and His disciples visiting the home of two sisters, Martha and Mary. Mary was sitting at the Lord's feet and learning from Him, while Martha was busily preparing things to serve to her guests. Martha was so distracted by what she was doing that she overlooked what was most important to do at the time.

Jesus is daily inviting and calling us to come to Him with our burdens. He is offering us a rest and peace that this world and even the results of our hard work can't offer. No amount of service can compare with the blessing of time with Him. For this is the best part of our life here on earth. Serving God in our calling is obviously important, but in all our daily preparations, let us not forget to daily prepare time with Jesus. Otherwise, we risk becoming like Martha, serving Jesus with a distracted devotion to Him.

In this 14 day devotional, you will be encouraged to continue in your devotional life with Christ. You will follow simple steps based on biblical references that will guide you to more fulfilling times with the Lord and produce a peaceful and merry heart. Then, as you grow in intimacy with Christ, you will find that your work and service will become less of a burden, as you "turn to God. . . that times of refreshing may come from the Lord" (Acts 3:19). Take a moment today to read the account of Jesus visiting the home of Martha and Mary in Luke 10:38-42.

1

DAY

Dine With Him

"Behold, I stand at the door and knock. If anyone hears My voice and opens the door, I will come in to him and will dine with him, and he with Me." Revelations 3:20

*M*artha was busily making preparations to serve Jesus and His disciples and working diligently to make sure He and they were comfortable. After all, Jesus Himself had come to dine with her at her home! She was anxious to make sure her work was prepared and that Jesus was pleased and attended to before she sat down to spend time with Him.

When Martha noticed that her sister, Mary, in her opinion, was doing nothing more than just sitting at the Jesus' feet, she became so bothered and upset that she declared to Jesus "Lord, don't you care that my sister has left me to do the work by myself? Tell her to help me!" (Luke10:40).

Mary was doing more than just sitting. She chose to sit at Jesus' feet **and** learn from Him. She chose, what Jesus said, was the one thing that was necessary. She knew that spending time with Jesus was the priority. Yes, He wanted to dine with them, but He wanted to give them food of eternal value. The Living Water, the Bread of Life, The Word of God, was in there presence, and in His presence she could find fullness of joy!

Like Martha, we often wait for all our work to be completed, all our boxes to be checked off, the feeling that we've done a good job, before we draw near to God and spend time with Him, when He is not waiting for us to be perfect or finish all our work first.

When we daily accept God's invitation to come to Him and dine with Him, we are choosing to receive His Word, the Bread of Life, and we are choosing to have an intimate relationship with Him. Martha had a relationship with Jesus, but Mary had an intimate relationship with Him. He wants you to open the door of your heart and sit down with him and let Him give you food of eternal value, a treasure which can not be taken away from you.

You are invited today and every day to come to Christ and dine with Him. Say yes and experience the blessing of abiding in Him, of intimacy with Him, and having a daily peace that surpasses all understanding, as you establish and continue a regular devotional time with your Savior.

Food For Thought

- *Would you consider yourself more of a Mary or a Martha type of person? Why?*
- *How important is devotional time with God to you?*
- *Do you have time set apart each day devoted to drawing near to God in prayer?*
- *If not, would you be willing to set apart time each day for time with Him?*

Plan Of Action

Think of how you can develop a balance between your work for Christ and your devotional time with Him. Take out your calendar, a journal, your Bible, and a favorite devotional and set them aside in a place that you think is best. Plan for a daily time, about the same time each day, to have a quiet time with the Lord. Don't let yourself miss out on a closer relationship with your Messiah, the Bread of Life!

Daily Notes

2
DAY

He Calls You By Name

*"He calls His own sheep by name and
leads them out." John 10:3*

*D*o you know that if you are a follower of Christ, He is daily calling your name, and that you are always on His mind and in His thoughts? He doesn't forget you or your needs for even one moment. He is your Creator and You are His masterpiece, and He thinks many precious thoughts about you. Psalm 139 is a beautiful description of the God Who knows you better than you know yourself and loves you more than you can imagine.

In our story, we read Jesus' response to Martha after she complains about her sister. He begins with, "Martha, Martha." Think of the last time someone said your name twice. It has usually been a time, for me at least, when someone who cared about me wanted to help me see things from a better perspective and guide me out of a wrong way of thinking or doing. When I hear my husband say, "Denise, Denise," it's often with a caring and concerned tone, and a guiding lesson.

This is how we can picture Jesus speaking to Martha. We read in Scripture that Martha, Mary and Lazarus were siblings and that they were very dear to Jesus. He considered them to be like family. When Jesus responded to Martha's complaint, He was doing so lovingly and with concern, and He did not just say her name, leaving her to complain, be distracted, and bothered. He called to her attention what she did not see that He did see. He wanted to guide her out of her wrong attitude and guide her into a better attitude. When you follow the Lord as your Shepherd every day, you can hear from Him what concerns Him. Psalm 23 comes to life as you let Him guide you and lead you to a place where your soul is quieted and restored. Then you can truly experience what it means to daily abide in Him.

Before the Bible was written, God sometimes spoke audibly. Now He speaks mostly through the revelation of the Bible, and the teaching, wisdom and guidance of the Holy Spirit. We can each now hear our Good Shepherd call us daily into His loving will.

Your Good Shepherd is calling you by name. He wants you to daily talk to Him about what burdens you. He wants to answer you through His Word, which has all things pertaining to life and godliness (2 Peter 1:3). God is calling you to be still and listen to His voice. Come to Him first with your burdens, for with tender concern He wants to speak to you and guide you. Your Savior wants to lead you out of any darkness and into the light so you can be at peace and be restored, because He cares for you.

I have used prayer methods, or prayer plans, during my devotions ever since I was a young believer. I choose to use prayer methods to help me to stay focused on God and His Word. One method I thought of to begin my devotional time has the acronym SOUL.

$\mathcal{S}$ is for **Sit and be Still**. Sitting can help us be still because we are less apt to move around and be distracted. Mary simply sat down at Jesus' feet and learned from Him. Let's follow her example.

$\mathcal{O}$ is for **Open your Bible**. There's nothing magical about where you turn in your Bible. God will lead you, if you are seeking Him. Many people use a current Bible study they are going through as a guide. During my devotions, I use either a Bible study or the One Year Bible, which has daily readings directly from the Bible for each day of the year. Psalm 119 is a good place to turn in the Bible, if you're not sure what to read. It's divided up into small sections according to the Hebrew alphabet. The psalmist shows his passion for God and for His Word throughout the Psalm.

$\mathcal{U}$ is for **Understand what you read**. This involves asking God to help you understand what you are reading in the Bible. There is little that we could understand from what we read without the God's guidance. I sometimes use a concordance to look up a word or phrase.

$\mathcal{L}$ is for **Listen to God speaking to you**. God is constantly speaking to us, even when we're not listening. We need to have the attitude of young Samuel, who said, "Speak, Lord, for your servant is listening." (1 Samuel 3:10).

Samuel was a boy when he had a very powerful encounter with God. He was the only child of Hannah, who prayed for many years that God would give her a son. She prayed earnestly, "Lord Almighty, if you will look upon my sorrow and answer my prayer and give me a son, then I will give him back to you. He will be yours for his entire lifetime" (1 Samuel 1:11). God eventually gave her a son, and Hannah did as she promised. She gave Samuel back to God to serve and live among the church leaders, and he ministered there under a priest named Eli.

One night, when he was sleeping, Samuel heard a voice calling his name. The Lord was calling Samuel's name but Samuel did not know it was God's voice. Samuel answered "Here I am" then ran to Eli and woke him up and said, "Here I am. You called me." This happened three times before Eli realized it was the voice of the Lord calling young Samuel. So Eli told Samuel "Go and lie down and if He calls you again, say '"Speak, Lord, for your servant is listening." Samuel went back to his bed then soon heard, "Samuel! Samuel!" Then Samuel said, "Speak, Lord, for your servant is listening" (Samuel 3:9,10). God now speaks to His people primarily through the written Word, the Bible. That is why it is so important to read the Word daily. May we have ears attentive to the voice of God, as young Samuel did, and say, "Speak, Lord, for your servant is listening."

- *Do you follow Jesus as your Shepherd and Guide? If you do, how do you seek His shepherding and guiding?*
- *What is your response when someone tries to show you how you can do things better?*
- *Would you say that using a prayer method helps you be more intimate with Christ or constrict your prayers?*
- *Would you be willing to try using a prayer method, if it would help you draw closer to God and help you have a more fulfilling devotional time with Him?*

Plan Of Action

Faith comes by hearing the Word of God (Romans 10:17). Quieting your soul daily before the Lord, and hearing Him speak to you through His Word will increase your faith. Apply the SOUL method of prayer today. Use a journal or the following page to write anything God reveals to you.

S is for *Sit and be Still*

O is for *Open your Bible*

U is for *Understand what you read*

L is for *Listen to God speak to you*

Daily Notes

3

Come Just As You Are

"*Trust in Him at all times, O people. Pour out your heart before Him.*" *Psalm 62:8*

*M*any people struggle with intimacy with Christ because they are worried they will say the wrong thing. Psalm 62:8 gives us a view of God as One who invites His people to lay it all out before Him. Martha seemed to have no problem with being real with Jesus. "She came to him and asked, 'Lord, don't you care that my sister has left me to do the work by myself? Tell her to help me!'" (Luke10:40). A few things are important to note here. First, she called Jesus "Lord" which means she had a right view of Him, as Lord. Also, Martha told her complaint to Jesus. Then, He answered her complaint by making her aware of her blindness to her sin. He showed her that she was so worried and bothered by so many things that she overlooked what was the most important thing at that moment. He spoke the truth to her in love.

Martha could have muttered her complaint under her breath, or possibly gossiped about her sister, but she chose to speak to her Lord about it. How often do we go to others about our complaints about one another rather than take it first to God? We could be missing out on seeing what Jesus wants to reveal to us about what our true motives are and where we are blind. Maybe it's time for us to have a reality check. Do we keep making excuses not to go to the Lord first with our prayers and concerns because we don't know what to say, or are we afraid of the truth of what God's Word might reveal about our hearts or say about our sin? Would we rather point to others' apparent wrongdoings and gossip about them rather than face our own issues with Christ?

Jesus said "Sanctify them in truth. Your Word is truth" (John 17:17). His motives could not be more pure in wanting us to be cleansed and sanctified from our sins. To sanctify means to be cleansed from sin and be made holy and pure. Nobody will ever love us like God. When we learn to be real with Christ, we realize that He will listen and respond to us and help us. Make a habit of going to God first with your complaints about your circumstances or a person. You might find out that you are going in the wrong direction, and you will always find that your Good Shepherd is there to "lead you beside quiet waters and restore (your) soul" and guide you "in the paths of righteousness for His Name's sake" (Psalm 23:2,3).

Yes, we need other Christians in our lives to be a shoulder to lean on, to counsel us, and guide us, but when people become substitutions for Christ, we border on, and sometimes blindly choose idolatry. We also run the risk of becoming bitter, angry, and deceived.

Mary also came to Jesus just as she was. She had nothing to offer him. She silently sat and listened to the Word of God. How hard it is for us busy women, when the situation seems to be calling for work and service, to take a moment to be still and listen to Him. We may even be influenced by the culture around us, from well-meaning busy churchgoers who have their own excuses as reasons not to have consistent devotional time with their Savior.

If times of refreshing come when we draw near to God, and if He has given us so much encouragement and admonition to pray and seek His ways, and if all things are laid bare and open to the eyes of the One with Whom we have to deal, is not now the time more than ever, to make sure we establish daily time of sitting at His feet and learning from Him? Peter said to Jesus, "Lord, to whom shall we go? You alone have the words of eternal life" (John 6:68). Jesus has words of eternal life to speak to you and me!

Some people also have a hard time drawing near to God because of the relationship they have or had with their earthly father. Did you know that your heart cries out "Abba Father" and that you are a beloved child to your Heavenly Father? Also, His Word promises that He will never leave or forsake you. He is a faithful and merciful Father, slow to anger and abounding in lovingkindness, and He is good to all who call on Him in truth (Galatians4:6, Hebrews 13:5, Psalm 145:8).

Another familiar acronym for prayer, which I learned as a young believer, is the **ACTS** method of prayer.

$\mathcal{A}$ is for **Adoration**. This is when we say or sing praises to God for Who He is. We read in Psalm 95:6, "Come let us worship and bow down. Let us kneel before the Lord our Maker." Whether you sit, kneel, or stand while you worship God, you are blessing your Maker.

$\mathcal{C}$ is for *Confession*. This is when we confess and repent from our sins. Daily confession and repentance is key to spiritual growth and maturity. Psalm 51 is a good guide for a repentant heart.

$\mathcal{T}$ is for *Thanksgiving*. This is when we thank God for forgiving our sins, and for all His provision, and for hearing and answering our prayers. The psalmist says in Psalm 100:4, "Enter His gates with thanksgiving and His courts with praise. Give thanks to Him and bless His Name."

$\mathcal{S}$ is for *Supplication*. This is when we offer up prayers for others and ourselves. "Stay alert with all perseverance and supplications for all the saints" (Ephesians 6:18). Jesus said, "Watch and pray, that you may not enter into temptation" (Matthew 26:41).

Food For Thought

- *When was the last time you went to God just as you are, pouring out your heart to Him?*
- *Does it help to write down what is in your heart?*

Plan of Action

Practice the ACTS method of prayer today, using a journal to write any praise or prayer that comes to mind.

A is for *Adoration*

C is for *Confession*

T is for *Thanksgiving*

S is for *Supplication*

Daily Notes

4

Take A Load Off Your Feet

*"Cast all your anxiety upon Him, because
He cares for you." 1 Peter 5:7*

*H*ave you ever felt like the weight of the world is on
your shoulders? If you have, or if you've had to
carry a burden that was too heavy for you to carry alone,
you can understand how anxiety and worry can develop
without someone to help you bear the burden.

Back in the time when Jesus was on earth, being a
fisherman was a common trade. Peter was a fisherman.
Casting a net into the water to get fish was a concept
his readers could find relatable. Our verse for this week
gives us an illustration of a fisherman casting a heavy,
burdensome mass of a soggy net trustingly upon the sea.
The net can represent your cares, your anxieties, whatever
is weighing you down. Thrust and trust them to the very
mighty arms that are supporting you. He cares about you
and wants you to take your trials and concerns to Him and
let Him carry you through them.

Martha certainly felt the weight of the world on her
shoulders. The Lord Jesus Himself and His disciples were
at her home and her sister was not lifting a finger to help

her! She even felt like Christ didn't care that Mary had left all the work to her. It was like she was carrying this heavy, burdensome weight of responsibility on her shoulders, with no one caring that she was doing it all by herself.

Nothing was farther than the truth. Jesus did care for Martha, enough so that He responded to her cry for mercy. "Martha, Martha. You are worried and upset about many things, but only one thing is necessary . . ." (Luke 10:41,42a). Jesus, in essence, took away the need for her to do anything more at the moment than be still and know that He is God. It was like He was telling her to take a load off her feet and lay it all down at His feet.

What a beautiful image of a Savior, Who not only gives us the gift of rest of mind and body through sleep, but offers rest for our souls during our times spent with Him. Yet while Jesus wants to give us rest, we must first come to Him with our weary hearts and heavy burdens. God has given us free will. He will not make or force us to come to Him, but if we make a practice of daily casting all our cares upon Him, we will find so much more than if we held it inside or went only to a person. When we make it a practice to go to Him first, we will find that no one can fill the longing of the weary heart like Jesus.

- *Do you usually go to God first to find wisdom, courage, and strength during a trial? Why?*
- *Who is a trusted friend you can call on during difficult times, to bear your soul, or to pray with you? Is this someone who will point you to God's principles?*

Plan Of Action

Songs with good biblical messages can help us draw nearer to Christ. Consider and pray over the words of this song as it applies to your walk with Christ:

"What a Friend we have in Jesus, all our sins and griefs to bear! What a privilege to carry everything to God in prayer!

O what peace we often forfeit, O what needless pain we bear, all because we do not carry everything to God in prayer."

Written by: Joseph Scriven

Daily Notes

_____

_____

_____

_____

_____

_____

_____

_____

_____

_____

_____

_____

_____

_____

_____

_____

_____

_____

_____

_____

_____

_____

_____

5

Sacrifice Your Time For His Time

"When you pray, go into your room, close the door and pray to your Father, who is unseen. Then your Father, who sees what is done in secret, will reward you." Matthew 6:6

J've heard many reasons from followers of Christ as to why they don't have a regular quiet time with Lord. One reasoning, based on the Scripture, which says "pray without ceasing" (1 Thessalonians 5:17), is that prayer should not be confined to a time and place. After all, we can put on the armor of the Spirit while we are driving, we can read a devotional during a lunch break, and we can lift others up in prayer as we are shopping at the market. While this is all true, we should not substitute set apart quiet time with God.

It's a sacrifice, but it's worth it. When we make a conscious effort to daily have time alone with God, we become more like Christ. Jesus often went to a solitary place to pray alone to the Father. There are many other reasons why the sacrifice of time in prayer is worth it. Here are a few. When we draw near to God during our daily devotions, the discipline of daily quieting our souls causes us to hear and understand God's Words more clearly. He wants to give us rest. He has words to say to us and teach us. Jesus said that what Mary did was necessary, so it is important to Him that we take time to stop working and listen to His Words.

God draws near to us when we draw near to Him. When we search our hearts daily and confess our sins, we walk in the light. God said to the Israelites, in Isaiah 30:15 "In repentance and rest is your salvation. In quietness and trust is your strength, but you were not willing." When we regularly and willingly submit to Christ by coming to Him, we experience quiet strength and rest for our souls. We see this picture in Psalm 23. We see the Good Shepherd leading his sheep beside still waters and restoring their souls. We see Him guiding them along the paths of righteousness, for His sake and His glory. We must be willing to submit to the process of quietness, rest, and repentance, in order to see His saving power in our daily lives.

God is blessed and glorified when we submit to Him in the process of prayer. We do well to set apart time to praise and worship Him, thank Him, put Him first by laying our burdens at His feet and trust Him with our cares.

Willingness to follow Christ involves personal sacrifice. In the case of intimacy with Christ and abiding in Him, it means sacrificing time to be with Him. In light of eternity, our time hear on earth is short, and the time we give to God in prayer daily is of eternal value.

Our verse for the day is a lesson from our Savior on having a quiet time, and the blessing of a reward for the one who takes time to pray. "But when you pray, go into your room, close the door and pray to your Father, who is unseen. Then your Father, who sees what is done in secret, will reward you" (Matthew 6:6). Notice that Jesus does not say "If you pray" but "When you pray". Also, He says to pray in your room with the door closed. The idea is to pray in a place where you are alone with God and there are no distractions, where no one and nothing is competing for your attention.

We also read that prayer is an act of faith. When you pray, you are displaying faith that the God you can't see can see you and hear your prayers. We read in Hebrews 11:6, "Without faith it is impossible to please Him, for everyone who comes to God must believe that He exits, and that He is a rewarder of those who seek Him." It is clear that Christ wanted to express that God sees the faith of those who take time to pray alone with Him.

Notice the action words of prayer and it's results to the one praying, to the prayer warrior. It's takes work and sacrifice to pray, but Jesus encourages us that God sees that you are taking the time to pray, and "what is done in prayer." He hears you praise and thank Him. He hears your requests for family and friends. He hears your heart's cry for healing and restoration. He sees it all and He hears it all, and He loves that you are coming to Him with it all, because He cares for you.

Lastly, we see the action God Himself will take when you take time daily to be alone with Him. God Himself will reward you for the work you do in prayer. Maybe it's time for us to see prayer as part of our work, part of our service and ministry. We all want to be rewarded for the things we do. Maybe we need to have more faith to please God, who we can't see, than to please people. The Pharisees were the religious elite in Jesus' day, who sought man's approval with all their outward works. Jesus is speaking against religious people-pleasing by calling His followers to pray in secret, and seek God and His approval.

Jesus prayed to the Father before He left the earth, and said, "This is eternal life, that they may know You, the only true God, and Jesus Christ, whom You have sent. I have glorified You on this earth, having accomplished the work which You have given me to do" (John 17: 3,4).

Our greatest rewards on this earth are to know God and glorify Him by accomplishing His will. Nothing will compare to the satisfaction and fulfillment you will have at the end of each day when you have sought Him in prayer and glorified Him with the work He has given you to do.

- *What part does time play as a factor in when and how long you can pray during the day?*
- *Are you willing to make a set plan for daily devotions with Christ?*
- *If you have a consistent daily quiet time, are you willing to take 5 more minutes each day in prayer?*

Plan Of Action

Write down in your calendar or journal 2 times during each day this coming week, starting tomorrow, that you can most likely spend time in prayer. That way if one doesn't work out, or you forget, the other time can be taken.

During your devotional time, practice both the SOUL and ACTS methods of prayer, and be ready to write down any verses or songs the Lord gives you and any new prayer requests and praise reports.

Daily Notes

_____

_____

_____

_____

_____

_____

_____

_____

_____

_____

_____

_____

_____

_____

_____

_____

_____

_____

_____

_____

_____

_____

6

Give Him Your Undistracted Attention

*"Martha was distracted by all the preparations
that had to be made." Luke 10:40*

*T*he culture around us offers us many definitions of
what a successful life should look like. Climbing
up the corporate ladder and keeping up with the Jones'
are two common phrases used for financial and societal
success. Yet we often disregard or overlook how we, as
Christians, may have a skewed definition of success. Favor
and faithfulness can be seen as common and legitimate
Christian terms for success, but if, in all our seeking to find
favor and be found faithful, we are waiting for the approval
of people rather than God's approval in doing His will, we
have truly lost the point.

In our familiar story, we find that the sister who found
favor with God was not the one who was being faithful in
human terms. It was the one who did God's will at that
moment, which was to be still and learn from Jesus. What
God wants us to do is to find our identity in Him, not in
the work He gives us to do. If our work is what drives us,
then we run the risk of idolatry and can be lead into a love
of money, pleasing others, and selfishness.

The book of James shows us a balance of a life of faith and works. Both are equally important parts of a Christian's character. Could you image having only faith and not works, or only works and not faith?

The question is not whether Martha was doing the right thing or not, it is whether her attitude was right in her service to Christ. It's not whether Mary should have been helping Martha, it's what her attitude was and whether she was showing genuine faith in Christ and discerning His will in that moment.

Sometimes our attitude needs to be adjusted and changed so that we can serve God with a clear conscience and a joyful heart. We read in Romans 12:2, "Do not be conformed to this world, but be transformed by the renewing of your mind, so that you may prove what the will of God is, that which is good, and acceptable, and perfect."

This transformation cannot come through service and ministry alone. It involves daily time spent with God, humbly worshipping Him, confessing our sins, thanking Him, offering up our needs to Him, and letting Him renew our spirit through His Word. Don't let the business of life and the time factor keep you from being daily renewed and refreshed in the Lord.

- *What are some things that distract you from time with God in prayer?*
- *What does giving Him your undistracted attention look like to you?*
- *Is a more organized, set apart place to offer your prayers something that will help you be less distracted?*
- *If so, consider working on a set apart, organized place and space to have your daily devotions.*

Plan Of Action

The psalmist said, "Your Word I have hidden in my heat that I might not sin against You" (Psalm 119:11).

God's Word will keep you from sin or sin will keep you from God's Word. Exam your heart and see if there is any sin that would keep you or distract you from reading God's Word daily. Write down what you find.

Daily Notes

7
DAY

Keep Calm And Lean On Him

"Do not fear, for I am with you. Do not anxiously look about you, for I am your God. I will strengthen you. Surely I will help you. Surely I will uphold you with my righteous hand." Isaiah 41:10

A nxiety breeds anxiety, and worry breeds worry. Is it any wonder that there are so many verses in the Bible about trusting God and having peace, rather than being anxious or afraid? We run the risk of many anxious thoughts finding their way into our hearts when we allow the smallest opening for a few of them. That is why we read in Phillipians 4:6 that we are to be anxious over **nothing.** Paul knew the power of anxiety but he also knew the power of the peace that overcomes.

Jesus told Martha that she was worried and bothered by so many things. Martha didn't *say* to Him that she was worried, but her actions and words gave her away. Jesus could see that she was anxious and worried about many things, including her sister. How many times have we blamed a person for our problems before looking inward? Jesus was looking into Martha's heart, revealing and making her aware of the root issues. He really did care about her, more than she knew. He wanted her to have peace, and turn from her anxieties. She become less and less calm, and more agitated and frustrated until she exploded.

At some point of our lives, we have all given ourselves over to anxiety. God wants us to trust Him first with all our heart, with all our burdens and concerns. He wants us to lean on His understanding (Proverbs 3:5). He knows what is best for us. Having a daily time set apart to talk to God and listen to Him is invaluable because, not only do we learn to go to Him first with all our concerns, but we developed the skill and discipline of listening to Him. We will start to experience the peace that surpasses all understanding when we lean consistently on on His perspective, on His Words of eternal life.

Learning to go to God, to trust Him, and lean on His understanding rather than your own, can best be taught in the school of quiet trust, as you draw near to Him in His presence. Jesus said, "Peace I leave with you; my peace I give you. I do not give to you as the world gives. Do not let your hearts be troubled and do not be afraid" (John 14:27). Trials and storms will come. Keep calm and lean on God. Lean on His everlasting arms, for your Heavenly Father longs to reveal His love and compassion towards you as you daily seek shelter and refuge in Him.

- *Is anxiety an issue for you?*
- *Have you experienced peace after praying for the things that bring about anxiety?*
- *Are you willing to calm your heart and let God console you when your anxious thoughts multiply in you?*

Plan Of Action

The psalmist said "When my anxious thoughts multiply within me, Your consolations delight my soul" (Psalm 94:19). He knew that he needed God's comfort and peace during troubled times and times of high anxiety. God wants to lead us to a place of peace and understanding. He wants to comfort us as we learn to be calm and lean on Him and His understanding during our trials.

Find and write at least 3 verses to think on when anxious thoughts arise or during trials that could bring about anxiety. Prepare your heart by reading these verses often.

Daily Notes

8
DAY

Listen To Words Of Wisdom

"Teach us to number our days, that we may present to You a heart of wisdom." Psalm 90:12

The beginning of our second week of devotions takes us beyond understanding the need for prayer. It takes us beyond the loving invitation of our Savior and the setting aside of our time and duties to be in His presence. It brings us to the place of experiencing what happens after we sit or kneel at His feet, to the discipline of listening to our Teacher instruct us in wisdom. Before Jesus left the earth to go back to Heaven, He said He would send us an Advocate and Helper, the Holy Spirit, to teach us all things and remind us of everything that Jesus taught us. He is with us in spirit through the Holy Spirit (John 16:7-15).

The Holy Spirit has been called a Counselor and Helper, Teacher and Guide. We draw near to God through the Spirit and God draws near to us through the Spirit. It is important to have the right view of God when we pray. When Jesus came to earth, He became the Word made flesh, God manifest as a man (John 1:14). When He went back to heaven, He remained the Word of God but was no longer flesh. He can not be physically with us as He was with Mary and Martha. He is now seated at the right hand of the Father (Mark 16:9).

Jesus said that He would always be with us through the Holy Spirit in us, and that the Spirit would reveal His Word to us. "But when the Spirit of truth, comes, He will guide you into all the truth, for He will not speak on His own initiative, but whatever He hears, He will speak, and He will disclose to you what is to come. He will glorify Me, for He will take of Mine and will disclose it to you" (John16:13,14).

God speaks to us in His Word is by revealing Himself and His will to us through the Holy Spirit in us. God has a word for each of us every day. He wants to lead us and guide us on right paths for His glory and for our good. He wants to convict us of sin and purify us to make us more like His Son. He wants us to walk in freedom and victory. That is why reading the Word of God during our quiet times is so very important, because that is where we find our Savior, ready to meet with us and dine with us and give us precious jewels of wisdom and understanding through the interpretation, help, and guidance of His Spirit.

Wisdom is the ability to use knowledge and understanding to think and act in such a way that common sense prevails and choices are beneficial and productive. 2 Peter 1:3 says, "His divine power has given us everything we need for a life and godliness, through our knowledge of Him who has called us by His own glory and goodness." God's Word is sufficient to guide us and lead us in the ways of wisdom, in ways that are productive and beneficial for our lives and for the lives of those in our sphere of influence.

If you want to be more wise and prudent in your decision making, reading and studying God's Word consistently is a key component to your growth in wisdom. We have all regretted making foolish decisions, and have come to realize that if we had only listened to counsel and direction from God's Word, the outcome of the situation would have been less of a loss and more of a victory.

We are told in Ephesians 5:17, "So then, do not be foolish but understand the Lord's will." Understanding God's will comes with reading and studying God's Word. The Holy Spirit will give you the wisdom you need for each day. When you take time to pray and read God's Word during a daily daily devotional time, God will be more than willing to guide you on the paths of righteousness. Quieting your soul is a big part of preparing your heart to listen to God's voice through His Word.

You will also be daily confessing and your sins, which is part of being sanctified. This will clear your heart and mind of the things that may have held you back from listening better. The point is that if you want to live daily in wisdom, seek the true source of wisdom. Seek God and seek to know and understand His ways, which are found in the Bible. Keep at your devotions every day, for this will discipline your mind and heart to keep praying, keep seeking, and keep making wise decisions throughout the day. Soon you will develop a heart of wisdom.

- *When was the last time you prayed to the Holy Spirit for wisdom or understanding before or when reading or studying Scripture?*
- *Do you sense that God reveals His will to you when you read the Bible? Do you interpret this as Him speaking to you?*
- *One mark of a mature Christian is wisdom. We read in James 1:5 that if we need wisdom, we should ask for it and God will gladly give it to us. Consider asking frequently for wisdom. It is yours for the taking.*

Plan Of Action

Read James 3:17. Write down each of these qualities of God's wisdom and pray over them to grow in you. Ask God to give you pure wisdom, then peaceable wisdom, then gentle wisdom, etc. As you grow in God's wisdom, you will find that the wisdom of the world will decrease and you'll better be able to understand and discern God's will for you.

Daily Notes

9
DAY

Give Him Your Burdens
And Lighten Up

"When my anxious thoughts multiply within me
Your consolations delight my soul." Psalm 94:19

*O*nce we accept our Savior's invitation to come to Him, and as we continue to do so, we experience a freedom and a lightening of the burdens that previously weighed us down. Whether it's sin we have been trying to shake off or worry and fear that keeps us from moving forward, our Savior wants to lighten our burdens by taking them from us and giving us a new song to sing, a song of freedom and forgiveness, of courage and victory.

The verse for this week tells of God's consolations delighting the soul that is weighted down with anxieties. When we let God comfort and console us, our souls are lifted by Him. We sense Him sympathizing with us. The comfort of the Holy Spirit becomes real as the goodness of the Father is revealed.

The psalmist says in Psalm 16:11, "You will make known to me the path of life; in Your presence is fullness of joy; in Your right hand there are pleasures forever."

The definition of delight is to take pleasure in, or enjoy. Jesus said that He is gentle and humble in spirit. When we come to Him with our heavy burdens, He displays His gentle love towards us. When we stay close to Him, His consolations delight our soul and He makes us know the path of life. As we know the path of life in His presence daily, we daily experience fullness of joy and the pleasures of His kingdom.

This is what God desires to give us. He wants us to find our delight in Him, be comforted by Him, and be guided by Him on the path of life. That is a great perspective to have when reading Phillipians 4:6,7, "Be anxious for nothing, but in everything, by prayer and supplication, with thanksgiving, let your requests be made know to God, and the peace of God, which surpasses all understanding, will guard your hearts and minds in Christ Jesus."

The implication is that a heart and mind at peace is protected. We also read is Isaiah 26:3, "You will keep him in perfect peace whose mind is stayed on You, because he trusts in You." As you continue in consistent daily devotions, your mind and heart will more readily be stayed and fixed on Jesus, and you will learn to trust God more and more each day.

- *What do you normally do if you get overwhelmed?*
- *Is giving God your burdens something you do on a regular basis? If not, or if it is difficult for you to do, would you consider writing down what weighs you down that you can give over to Him?*
- *Read Phillipians 4:6. Write down the instructions, what the promise of peace is like, and how it will protect you.*

Plan Of Action

Think of any burdens of anxiety or worry or any other unnecessary burdens you may carry daily that you can give to Jesus now. Consider taking them out of your hands and placing them into Christ's hands. Write them down if it helps to fully let go.

Now you can listen more clearly to your Savior's words when you sit at His feet and learn about the paths of life and righteousness. You will be less weighted down and even lifted up as He gives you the strength and courage to live out what He teaches you, as you taste and see that He is good!

Daily Notes

10
DAY

Develop A "Merry" Heart

*"A merry heart is good medicine but a crushed
spirit dries up the bones." Proverbs 15:13*

*O*riginally, to be merry did not imply merely being
joyful and happy but to be strong and brave. It was
in this sense that brave soldiers were called merry men, as
in "Robin Hood And His Merry Men." The word merry
later carried with it the double meaning of might and joy,
and is used both ways in Scripture.

The best verse to go with the double definition of this
merriment that we, as Christians, are called to be, is found
in Nehemiah 8:10, "The joy of the Lord is your strength."
We also read in Psalm 118:14, "The Lord is my strength
and my song, and He has become my salvation."

These verses imply that strength in the Lord
accompanies joy, and joy accompanies strength. That is
why, when you sing praises to God and worship Him, you
find yourself getting stronger in your spirit. Likewise,
when you become stronger in your walk with the Lord,
your joy increases as you become more courageous and
successful in defeating sin and living a victorious life.

Daily time set apart with Christ, where you worship

Him, listen to Him, thank Him, confess and repent from sin, offer up your needs, and spiritually prepare yourself for the day, is a huge part of the building up of this kind of merry heart, a heart full of joy and peace, courage and strength.

Thankfulness is another way that we can develop a merry heart. In 1 Thessalonians 5:18 we read, "In everything give thanks, for this is God's will for you in Christ Jesus." Another place where we read what God's will is for us in Christ Jesus is 1 Thessalonians 5:3, "This is God's will for you, your sanctification." Part of doing God's will is submitting to the process of sanctification by always being thankful. Thankfulness also brings about contentment and peace, and dispels jealousy and greed.

When Jesus warned that in this world we will have trials and tribulation, the word of encouragement He used after that was very similar to the word merry. The most accurate versions of the Bible differ in the word used here. The NASB says that Jesus said "Take courage." The King James Version says "Be of good cheer" (John 16:33). Courage and cheer are two different words, but in light of being merry, they are one in the same.

Did you notice that we did not hear a word from Mary? She was quietly being strengthened in her heart and spirit as she sat at Jesus' feet and learned from Him. Our Proverb for the day says that a merry heart is good medicine. God is waiting to strengthen your heart, restore health to your wounds, and heal you. He wants you to be of good courage and of good cheer, for He is your victory!

- *Would you say that you tend to be more courageous or fearful? Why?*
- *Would you say that you tend to be more joyful or bitter? Why?*
- *Given what you have read about the correlation of joy in the Lord and strength in the Lord, what steps will you take to develop more of a "merry" heart?*

Plan Of Action

Write down 5 reasons why you are thankful. Thankfulness helps us to be content with what we have and can dispel discouragement. Go over this list again later on in the day.

God commanded Joshua to be very strong and very courageous (Joshua 1:7). The prophet Nehemiah encouraged the Israelites seeking God by saying, "The joy of the Lord is your strength" (Nehemiah 8:10b). Think of and and write down any relationships or situations in your life that you need great strength and courage to face. Ask the Lord for wisdom, courage and strength to deal with that person or situation, then go forward trusting, praising and thanking God for His provision and help!

Daily Notes

_____

_____

_____

_____

_____

_____

_____

_____

_____

_____

_____

_____

_____

_____

_____

_____

_____

_____

_____

_____

_____

_____

11
DAY

Sit And Learn With Your Sisters

"We all, with unveiled face, behold, as in a mirror, the glory of the Lord, are being transformed into that same image from glory to glory. . ." 2 Corinthians 3:18

*M*ary and Martha were in the presence of the Lord Jesus Christ, God in human form! If any generation saw God unveiled, it would be the generation who beheld Him as the perfect God Incarnate, whose very glory was the glory the Father, and that glory was with Him wherever He went. Both of the women knew enough about who He was to know that He deserved the greatest honor, yet only Mary chose to draw near to Him as her Master Teacher.

Her example has been a reference over the years as to why God wants His people to draw near to Him, spend time with Him and learn from Him. Jesus pointed to her as an example for her sister and for us to follow. We also can learn how to pray from one another. Prayer is not only necessary in our intimacy with Christ, but it also is an integral part of our spiritual warfare as believers. Together, we are part of God's army, for the advancement of His kingdom.

Putting on the armor of the Spirit, submitting our thoughts captive in obedience to Christ, being filled with the Spirit, confession of sins, and other important disciplines of prayer ought to be encouraged, taught, and shared by sisters in Christ on a regular basis.

Based on what I have heard Christians say over the years, most don't have a regular time set apart for Him. It is not seen as a priority to them. Yet, in reference to Mary's act of submission at the feet of Jesus, He called it necessary and good. Martha needed to learn from her sister what her priorities needed to be. If your priority is God first, then give Him the first fruits of your day.

When we sit and learn about God's Word and pray together, we are transformed together. Our daily devotions will be richer because we will have been in fellowship with Him and one another, "for where two or three are gathered together in My Name," He said, "there I am in their midst" (Matthew 18:20).

Family devotions are also a very important discipline. While we are in the family of God and each member is to participate in the building up of the Body of Christ, the priority of our time and energy is usually dedicated towards the responsibilities we have toward our families at home. Whether you are a wife, mother, daughter, or sister to someone in your home, or all four, having daily family devotions with the members of your home can become a cherished and valuable time together. How wonderful it would be if every family consistently praised and thanked God together, read His Word, confessed their sins to one another, and prayed for one another!

There is one last acronym that I use during my devotional time. It is the one I use to wrap up my quiet time before I head out to face the world. Since I will be serving and influencing people every day, I thought of a final method that would involve preparing my character (my thoughts, words, attitudes and actions) for the day ahead. The acronym is FAITH.

F is for *Fruit of the Spirit.* We are told that if we walk by the Spirit we will not gratify the desires of the flesh (Galatians 5:16). Seek daily to be filled with the fruit of the Spirit and seek to walk in them throughout the day. "The fruit of the Spirit is love, joy, peace, patience, kindness, goodness, faithfulness, gentleness and self-control" (Galatians 5:22).

A is for *Armor of God.* We are told to be strong in the Lord and in the strength of His might, and to daily put on the armor of God. "Therefore, put on the full armor of God, so that when the day of evil comes, you may be able to stand your ground, and after you have done everything, to stand. Stand firm then, with the belt of truth buckled around your waist, with the breastplate of righteousness in place, and with your feet fitted with the readiness that comes from the gospel of peace. In addition to all this, take up the shield of faith, with which you can extinguish all the flaming arrows of the evil one. Take the helmet of salvation and the sword of the Spirit, which is the word of God" (Ephesians 6:10-17).

I is for *In Everything Give Thanks.* 1 Thessalonians 5:18 says, "In everything gives thanks, for this is

God's will for you in Christ Jesus." You can consider this as preparing yourself in your speech for the day. Other versus on what our speech should be like are Colossians 4:6 and Ephesians 4:29.

T is for *Thoughts captive to Christ.* We are told to submit our thoughts captive in obedience to the authority of Christ (2 Corinthians 10:5). We are also given a set of thoughts on which to think. "Whatever things are true, honest, just, pure, lovely, of good repute, if there be any excellence, anything worthy of praise, let your mind dwell on these things" (Phillipians 4:8). God is the author of peace, not confusion, and He will keep in perfect peace the man or woman who trusts Him and whose mind is focused on Him (1 Corinthians 14:33, Isaiah 26:3).

H is for *Holiness is the goal.* The will of God is our sanctification, which simply means to be made holy. We are to partner with God in this process. Peter admonished his readers in 1 Peter 1:15, "Be holy in all you do." Apart from Christ, this is impossible. Jesus Himself said, "I am the Vine. You are the branches. He who abides in Me and I in him, he bears much fruit, for apart from Me you can do nothing" (John 15:5). There is no way we could do what God has called us to do without abiding in Him, and I can't think of a better way to discipline my heart to abide in Christ than to spend time with Him, listening to Him, talking to Him, and seeking Him.

It has been said that failing to plan is planning to fail. Having been a Christian for long enough, I have found that when I am prepared for the day, with it's responsibilities, trials, battles, and ultimate victories, God is glorified. I find that I can draw on the wisdom, filling, and strength that my King gave me when He showed me His will and gave me His blessing for my day. The Psalmist said, "As the eyes of servants look to the hand of their master . . . so our eyes look to the Lord our God until He is gracious to us" (Psalm 123:2). Look to and listen to the Lord daily, just as Mary did, and He will bless you with wisdom, strength, mercy and favor.

Daily Notes

_____

_____

_____

_____

_____

_____

_____

_____

_____

_____

_____

_____

_____

_____

_____

_____

_____

_____

_____

_____

_____

_____

_____

- *Would you say that your daily devotions are fulfilling?*
- *What do you do during your daily devotions?*
- *Is there a Christian in your home with whom you could do a few daily devotions each week?*

Plan Of Action

Remembering the spiritual gear to "put on" can be made easier through the acronym FAITH. We need faith that God will help us carry out His will each day. Practice the FAITH plan of prayer today.

F is for *Fruit of the Spirit (Galatians 5:22,23)*

A is for *Armor of the God (Ephesians 6:13-17)*

I is for *In everything give thanks (1 Thess. 5:18)*

T is for *Thoughts captive to Christ (2Cor.10:5, Phil.4:8)*

H is for *Holiness is the goal (1Peter 1:15)*

Daily Notes

12
DAY

Live A Balanced Devotion To Him

*". . . walk in a manner worthy of the Lord, pleasing Him
in all respects, bearing fruit in every good work and
increasing in the knowledge of God." Colossians 1:10*

*T*he management of our time is a vital factor in our
lives and ministries. We can have a timely schedule
thrown off by something as simple traffic. So making the
most of our time each day is of essence. Whatever your
responsibilities are, time is a factor that has to be dealt with
wisely. Once again, we are reminded of the word of the
psalmist, "Teach us to number our days that we may gain a
heart of wisdom" (Psalm 90:12). The woman who manages
her time wisely will find more success in her service than
if she was careless with her time.

Setting aside precious time daily to draw near to God
is a goal every believer should have in their routine. God
is constantly speaking to His people. If we're not careful
to practice the virtue of listening to Him speak, we could
miss out on a timely Word from God and start to lose the
spiritual sense of listening to the Holy Spirit.

When I take time to listen to God speak to me and give
Him my cares and burdens for the day, I sense a spiritual

release of carrying the burdens of the day alone. I have supernatural help and strength to face the day's challenges. That is why I encourage people to have their quiet time in the morning, if possible.

A fulfilling and productive quiet time usually consists of listening to God speak to us through His Word, praising Him, confession and repentance of sins, thanking God, supplication, and the preparation of the mind and heart for the day ahead. Breaking up the process of prayer into time fragments is ok and better than not praying at all, but there is a certain fulfillment and freedom of the soul when we come to Christ first thing in the morning, and give Him the concerns of our day. When we let Him refresh us and prepare us, through His Word and prayer, we can experience an easier and lighter load that He wants to carry with us. Then our service to Him will be more fulfilling, and we will have more peace, having spent quality time with the One Who made us and holds our lives in His hands.

The psalmist said "Give ear to my words, O Lord. Consider my groaning. Heed the sound of my cry for help, my King and my God, for to you I pray. In the morning, O Lord, You will hear my voice. In the morning I will order my prayer to You and eagerly watch" (Psalm 5:1-3). Why the morning? What better time is there to seek God's help and lay out your requests and burdens to Him than in the morning? Just as the psalmist needed God's help, we all need to seek His comfort and guidance. When we give Him the day ahead of us, we can go forward in peace, knowing that we have surrendered our cares and concerns into the hands of our loving and mighty Father.

- *Is having devotional time with God in the morning something you do or have done regularly in the past?*
- *Do you find it difficult to complete your devotions?*
- *Do experience peace and comfort, and maybe are less heavy hearted after you spend time with the Lord?*

Plan Of Action

Jesus wants to lift us up and help carry the burdens of the day. I suggest trying to make time with the Lord early in the day a priority. Making it timely and fulfilling is key. In light of making the most of our time, consider using all three methods of prayer that have been discussed in this book.

Start with SOUL, then ACTS, then FAITH. A good way to remember this is "soul acts of faith". Use your journal to jot down any verses, prayers, praise reports, etc. May God richly bless your time with Him!

Daily Notes

13
DAY

The Heart Of The Daily Devoted Woman

"No servant can serve two masters, for either he will hate the one and love the other, or he will be devoted to one and despise the other. You cannot serve God and wealth." Luke 16:13

It was obvious that the Pharisees loved money, but Jesus was not only talking to the Pharisees when he said the words above. He was also warning His disciples and anyone else hearing Him about the love of money. If we are going to serve God, we need to daily be keeping our own hearts in check against idolatry.

Serving God in our particular ministry and calling can be very rewarding, but if we are not careful, it can lead to pride, selfishness, and the love of money. The servant of God can also become very weary, and if the work is not accompanied with the strength of Christ and in a relationship to Him, she can become tired and weak from serving in her own strength. Jesus said "If you remain in Me and I in you, you will bear much fruit. Apart from Me, you can do nothing" (John 15:5). Jesus meant that we cannot produce genuine spiritual fruit on our own. We need to abide in Him. We need to walk with Him in the light.

This is where prayer and time spent alone with God daily is so vital to a healthy spiritual life and ministry. When you develop this kind of spiritual vitality, you will more often experience the positive effects of a single-hearted devotion to Christ. You will have more peace and will serve God more joyfully because you will have given Him your day, and set your mind on Him early in the day. The words of Paul to the Colossians will be more real in our lives. "Whatever you do, do your work heartily, as for the Lord rather than for men, knowing that from the Lord you will receive the reward of the inheritance. It is the Lord Christ whom you serve" (Colossians 3:23,24).

In this fast-paced world, where the love of money and self are main influences, daily devotional time to check our hearts is vital and necessary. I'd like to reiterate what I wrote in Day 5, titled "Sacrifice Your Time For His Time," regarding the reasons why the time we sacrifice to God in prayer is so valuable.

When we make a conscious effort to daily have time alone with God, we become more like Christ. Jesus often went to a solitary place to pray alone to the Father. There are many other reasons why the sacrifice of time in prayer is worth it. Here are a few. When we draw near to God during our daily devotions, the discipline of daily quieting our souls causes us to hear and understand God's Words more clearly. He wants to give us rest. He has words to say to us and teach us. Jesus said that what Mary did was necessary, so it is important to Him that we take time to stop working and listen to His Words.

God also draws near to us when we draw near to Him. When we search our hearts daily and confess our sins, we walk in the light. God said to the Israelites, in Isaiah 30:15, "In repentance and rest is your salvation. In quietness and trust is your strength, but you were not willing." When we regularly and willingly submit to Christ by coming to Him, we experience quiet strength and rest for our souls. We see this picture in Psalm 23. We see the Good Shepherd leading his sheep beside still waters and restoring their souls. We see Him guiding them along the paths of righteousness, for His sake and His glory. We must be willing to submit to the process of quietness, rest, and repentance, in order to see His saving power in our daily lives.

God is blessed and glorified when we submit to Him in the process of prayer. We do well to set apart time to praise and worship Him, thank Him, put Him first by laying our burdens at His feet and trust Him with our cares.

Willingness to follow Christ involves personal sacrifice. In the case of intimacy with Christ and abiding in Him, it means sacrificing time to be with Him. In light of eternity, our time hear on earth is short, and the time we give to God in prayer daily is of eternal value.

Your service to Christ and the amount and effort you put into providing for your family and in your ministry is of great value. As you serve your Master, keep in mind that He is constantly speaking and waiting for you to draw near and listen to Him. Truly we can say as Simon Peter said to our Savior," "Lord, to Whom shall we go? You alone have the words of eternal life" (John 6:68). Keep going to Him daily and serving Him with the grace, strength and wisdom He gives you. He will increase as you decrease, and the world will see Christ in you, the Hope of glory, for not only will you know about God but you will **know** God.

Food For Thought

- *Do you treasure and value a daily devotional time with Jesus more than before reading this book? Has this book helped you have a better sense of the eternal value of a consistent daily devotional time with God?*

- *The psalmist said, "Your Word I have treasure in my heart, that I may not sin against You" (Psalm 119:11). Do you treasure God's Word in your heart enough to study it and memorize versus? Are you reminded of His Word when you are tempted to sin or during a trial?*

Plan Of Action

Consider drawing, making, or buying two jewelry boxes or two mason jars. Write down verses and prayer requests on small cards that you want to remember and keep in your heart and mind throughout your day and week. Once you've memorized a verse or a prayer request has been answered, remove the card from the box or jar. You can also simply write the verses and prayer requests in your journal. You'll be amazed at how much of God's Word you can remember and how He answers prayers!

Daily Notes

14

An Eternal And Priceless Treasure

"Do not store up for yourselves treasures on earth,
where moths and rust destroy, and where thieves
break in and steal...For where your treasure is,
there your heart will be also." Matt.6:19,21

*W*hat would you say do you treasure the most? What
makes it so valuable to you? Few people think often
of what they treasure the most. Yet it's good to get an
inventory of where the heart is every now and then. God
cares so much for us that He uses a the relatable concept
of a treasure in the verse above to guide us into treasuring
Him and a relationship with Him more than anything.

Our Savior said, "This is eternal life, that they may
know You, the only true God, and Jesus Christ whom
You have sent" (John 17:3). That means that we don't have
to wait until we're in heaven to have a relationship with
the Father and the Son. We can know Him here on earth
through the guidance of the Holy Spirit. God longs for us,
His children, to know not just about Him, but to know
Him intimately. Bible study is so important in knowing
who God is, who we are to God, and how to obey Him.
The knowledge of God and His Word will help us stay on

the right path. The psalmist said, "Thy Word is a lamp into my feet and a light unto my path" (Psalm 119:105). Yet the knowledge of God, if not accompanied by a relationship with Him, can lead to pride and a false sense of security.

Jesus said, "Seek first the kingdom of God and His righteousness, and all these things will be added unto you" (Matthew 6:33). He said this after teaching about the uselessness of worry. When we seek God's kingdom and righteousness before everything else, He provides for all our needs.

The eternal and priceless treasure Mary found at the feet of Jesus was the Lord Himself, and spending time with Him. When Jesus said to Martha that Mary chose the good part which would not be taken away from her, He was essentially saying that she was storing up for herself a treasure of time spent with her Savior here on earth. The desire of her heart was to be with and learn from her Good Shepherd.

Any relationship, whether husband and wife, parent and child, or a friendship, is made healthier and stronger with frequent quality time together. When you spend consistent quality time with God daily, you are storing up a valuable treasure in the storehouse of heaven of an intimate relationship with your Maker!

Christ's invitation to us is just as real as it was when we first started this devotional journey. He says, "Come to Me, all you who are weary and heavy laden, and I will give you rest. Take My yoke upon you and learn from Me, for I am gentle and humble in heart, and you will find rest for your souls" (Matthew 11:28-30). Say yes again and again to Jesus, my sister, and you will find that only One can fill your life with genuine peace and fulfillment.

- *How has this book been helping you in your devotional time with God?*
- *Is there something you plan to apply from this book that you have not yet applied in your devotions?*
- *How have you come to know Christ more intimately since reading this devotional?*

Plan Of Action

Now that you have been practicing having consistent daily devotions, you can share with others what God has been teaching you during your times with Him. Jesus said, "What I tell you in the darkness, speak in the light; and what you hear whispered in your ear, proclaim upon the housetops" (Matthew 10:27). He wants you to share with others what He discloses to you during your time with Him. It is meant to be shared.

Start sharing with people what God is speaking to you in your devotional times. Share what you are learning about having fulfilling devotions. Your testimony can inspire others and encourage them to seek and know the Lord.

Daily Notes

Quick Tips For Fulfilling Devotions

- *Commit to a regular time and place to have your daily devotions. Make it your goal to meet with God during this time every day.*
- *Have a Bible, devotional, and journal at or near the place you will have your devotional time.*
- *Consider including the following tools during your Bible reading time:*
  - *The One Year Bible, which contains 365 daily readings of the Bible, each day broken up into 4 readings from the Old Testament, New Testament, Psalms, and Proverbs.*
  - *A Study Bible*
  - *A Bible Concordance*
- *Consider using the SOUL ACTS of FAITH plan for a more fulfilling, timely, and productive devotional time. It is written out out on the next page.*
- *Make sure you read from the actual Bible during your devotional time. "All Scripture is inspired by God and profitable for teaching, reproof, discipline, and training in righteousness" (2 Timothy 3:16).*

The "*SOUL ACTS* of *FAITH*" Plan:

S is for *Sit and be Still*

O is for *Open your Bible*

U is for *Understand what you read*

L is for *Listen to God speaking to you*

A is for *Adoration*

C is for *Confession*

T is for *Thanksgiving*

S is for for *Supplication*

F is for *Fruit Of The Spirit*

A is for *Armor Of God*

I is for *In Everything Give Thanks*

T is for *Thoughts captive to Christ*

H is for *Holiness is the goal*

You will find a detailed description of each of these plans on pages 11,18,52, and 53.

Conclusion

$\mathcal{M}$odels for prayer are not a new concept. Jesus Himself gave a basic model for prayer, as described in the following versus from Luke 11:1-4:

"One day Jesus was praying in a certain place. When He finished, one of His disciples said to Him, 'Lord, teach us to pray, just as John taught his disciples.'" He said to them, "When you pray, say:

"'Father, hallowed be Your Name.
Your kingdom come.
Give us each day our daily bread.
Forgive us our sins,
For we also forgive everyone who sins against us.
And lead us not into temptation.'"

Prayer is ultimately about having a relationship with God and intimately knowing Him. Make and take time to grow in this priceless and eternal gift. May God bless your walk with Him!

Notes

Notes

Notes